Family
Blessing
Book

"Twinkle" Marie Porter-Manning

Matrika Press

$\mathcal{M}$atrika $\mathcal{P}$ress

Matrika Press
P.O. Box 115
Rockwood, Maine 04478
Editor@MatrikaPress.com

www.MatrikaPress.com

Dedication

To my family and to yours,

May we treasure the wisdom we gain from each other and may we pass it on from generation to generation, ever growing stronger, ever becoming more loving. May we learn from our mistakes and, together, may we celebrate our triumphs.
May we be a blessing to each other.
Always and All ways.

Ed Porter
I love you.
I cherish the family we've created together.
You are my dream come true.

In loving memory of
Riley Dai Callin

Introduction

Blessing Books are created by "Twinkle" Marie Porter-Manning and are a source of intentional inspiration to be used to record personal messages to the owner of the Blessing Book. These mementos and keepsakes can be used in rituals, celebrations and communions as well as for self-reflection and documentation of one's innermost thoughts, feelings and beliefs. At the heart of Blessing Books is the desire to share sentiments, messages and stories that we can draw upon as sources of comfort and a reminder that we are loved. This Blessing Book was created with the family in mind.

How to Use the Family Blessing Book:

Whether you are in a group gathering, or pass the book from one family member to another over a period of time, have each person select a word or phrase that is meaningful to them. Place the word or phrase at the top of selected page. Use the content space provided to describe its significance. Be sure to write your name in the designated space at the bottom of the page so your family knows this message is from you! This book can be used in times of joy or in times of sorrow.

The *Family Blessing Book* can also be filled out by a solitary family member who wishes to have a book filled with their own reflections for their family. Indeed, each family can have multiple Family Blessing Books that each hold the author's unique insights and wisdom. Cherished memories and words of gratitude can become themes throughout Blessing Books, as well as drawing upon your family's unique etymology.

Wherever you are on your journey, may this Blessing Book serve you well.

For more resources and rituals to accompany this book, including Blessing Stones, visit: MatrikaPress.com/Blessing-Books

This Blessing Book belongs to:

_____

Occasion:

_____

Date:

_____

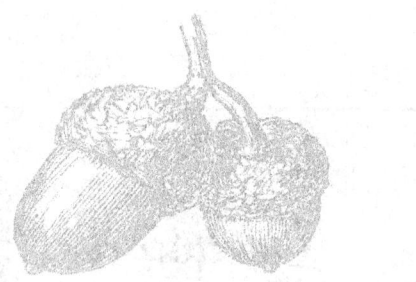

Table of Contents

14. _____

15. _____

16. _____

17. _____

18. _____

19. _____

20. _____

21. _____

22. _____

23. _____

24. _____

25. _____

26. _____

27. _____

28. _____

29. _____

30. _____

31. _____

32. _____

33. _____

34. _____

35. _____

36. _____

37. _____

38. _____

39. _____

40. _____

41. _____

42. _____

43. _____

44. _____

45. _____

Written by: _____

Written by: _____

Written by: _____

Written by: _____

Written by: _____

Written by: _____

Written by: _____

Written by: _____

Written by: _____

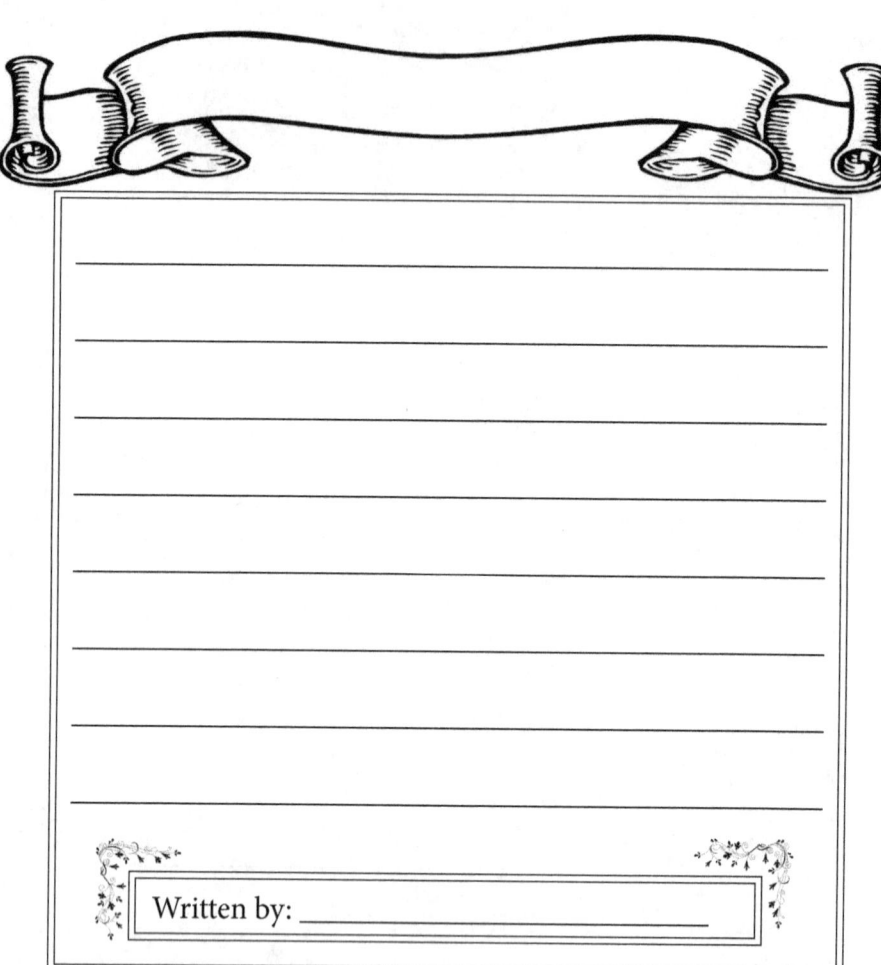

Written by: _____

Written by: _____

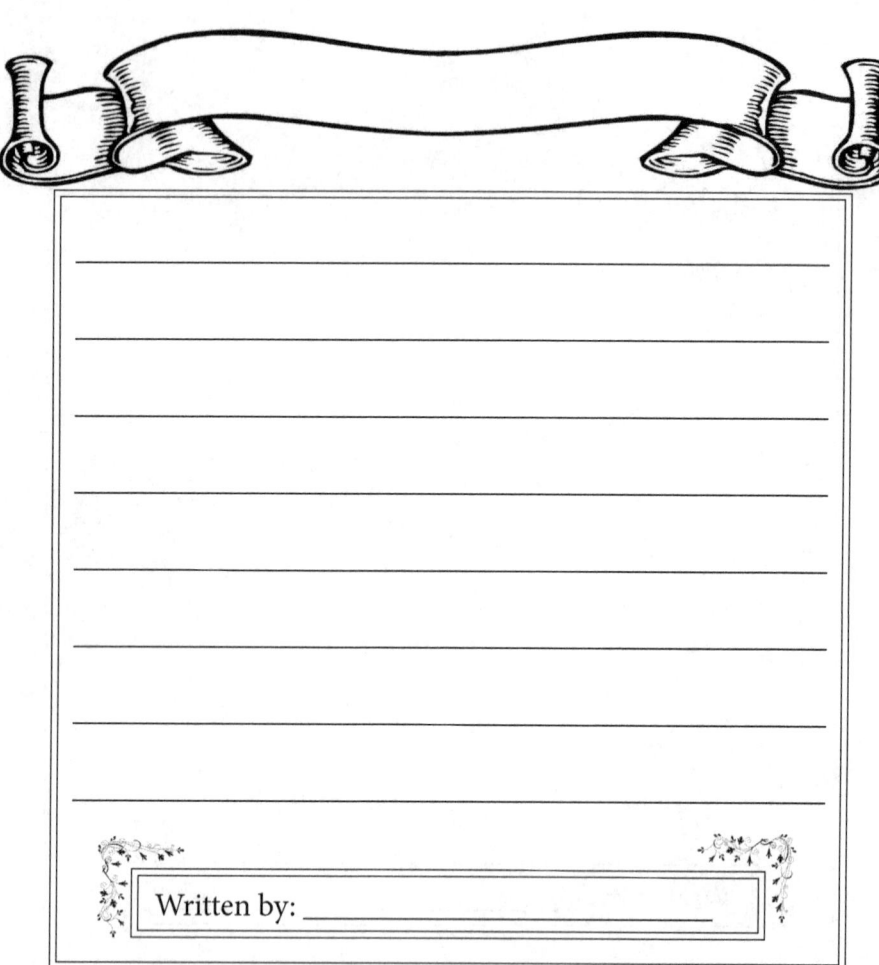

Written by: _____

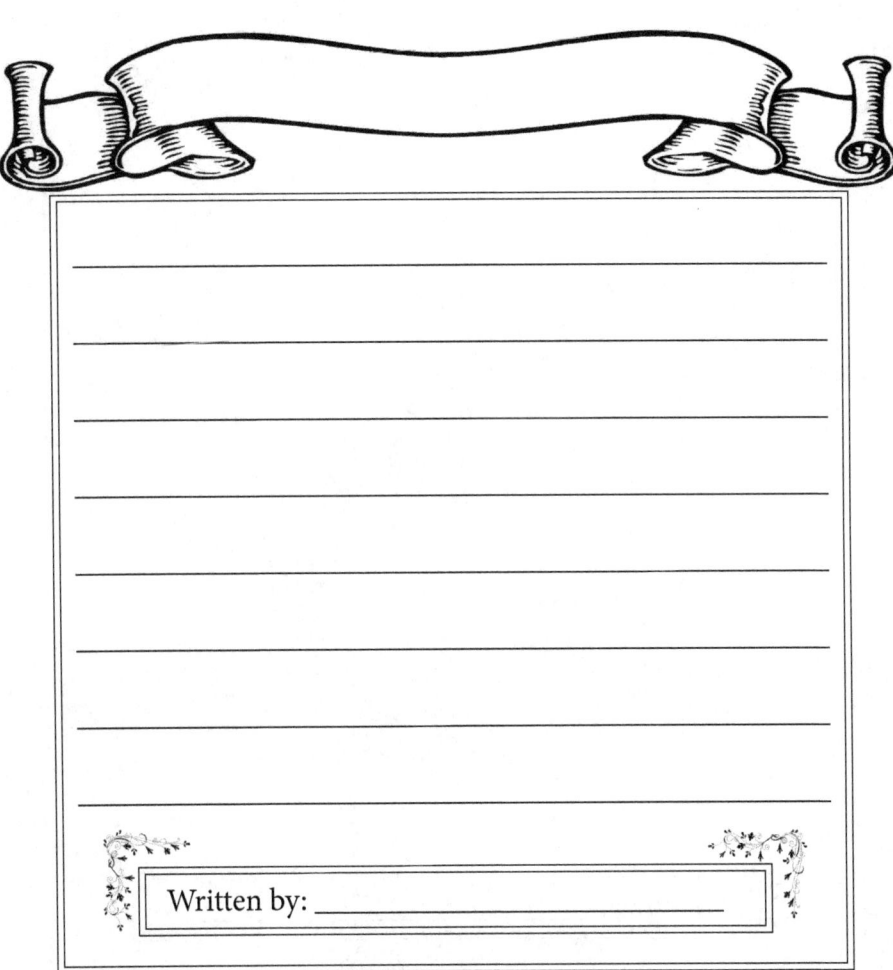

Written by: _____

Written by: _____

Written by: _____

Written by: _____

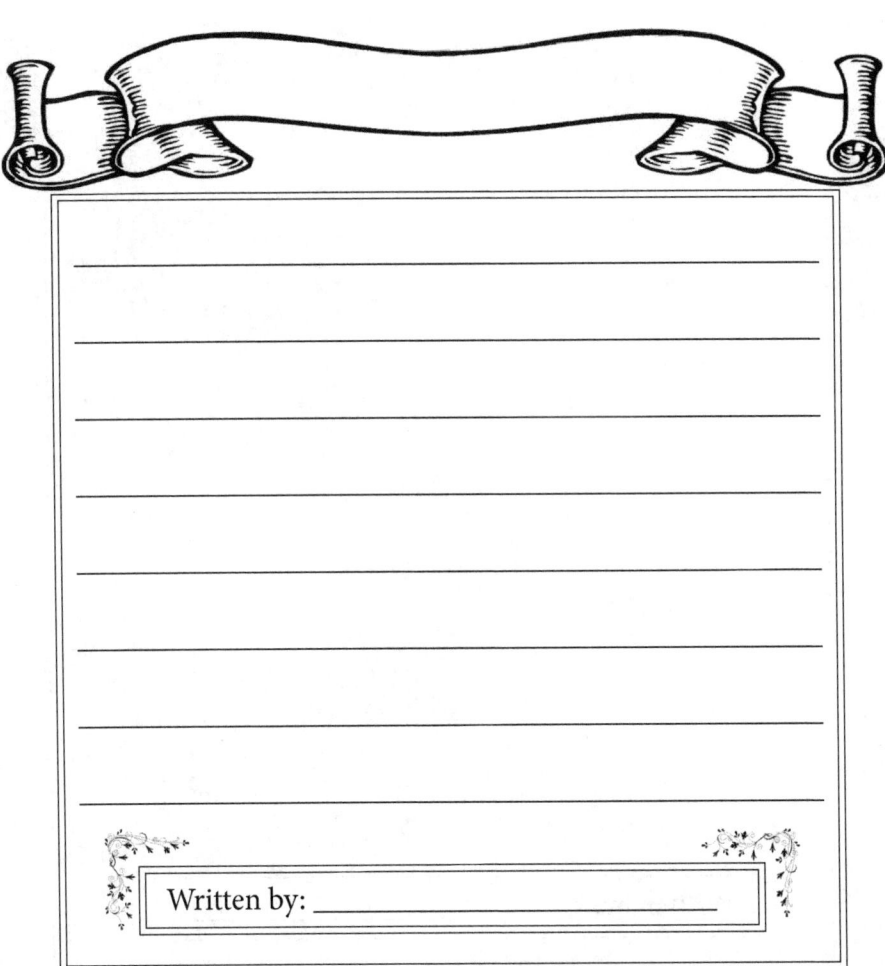

Written by: _____

Written by: _____

Written by: _____

Written by: _____

Written by: _____

Written by: _____

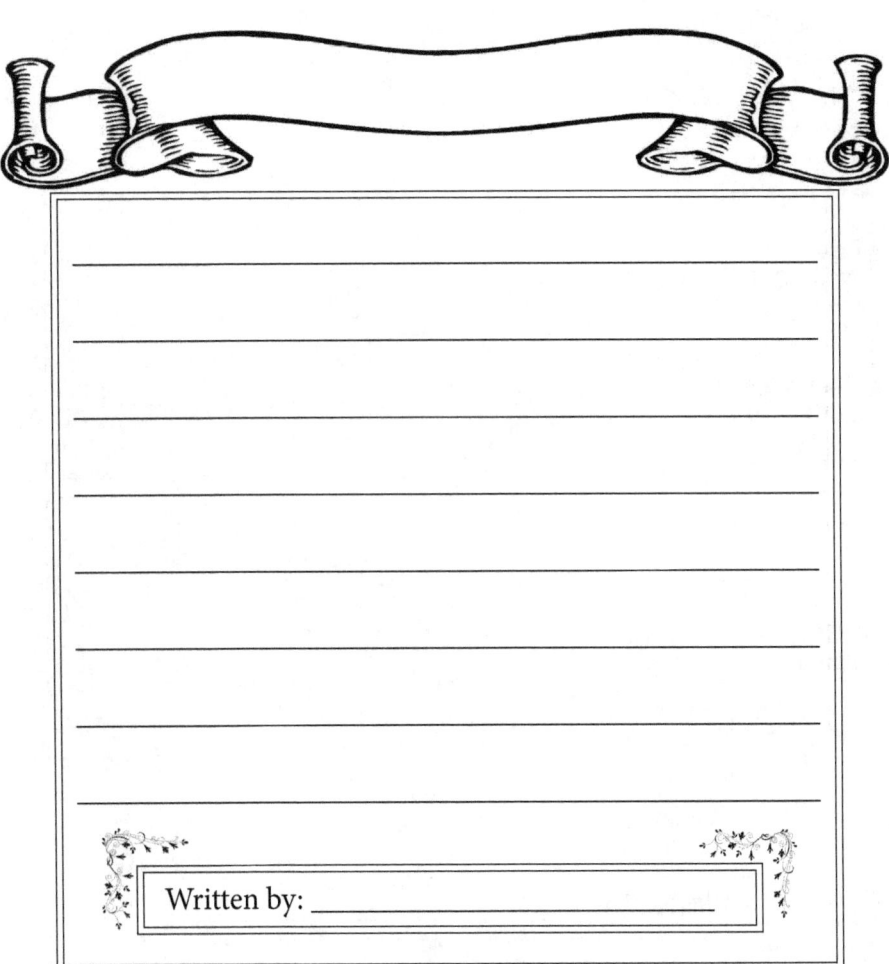

Written by: _____

Written by: _____

Written by: _____

Written by: _____

Written by: _____

Written by: _____

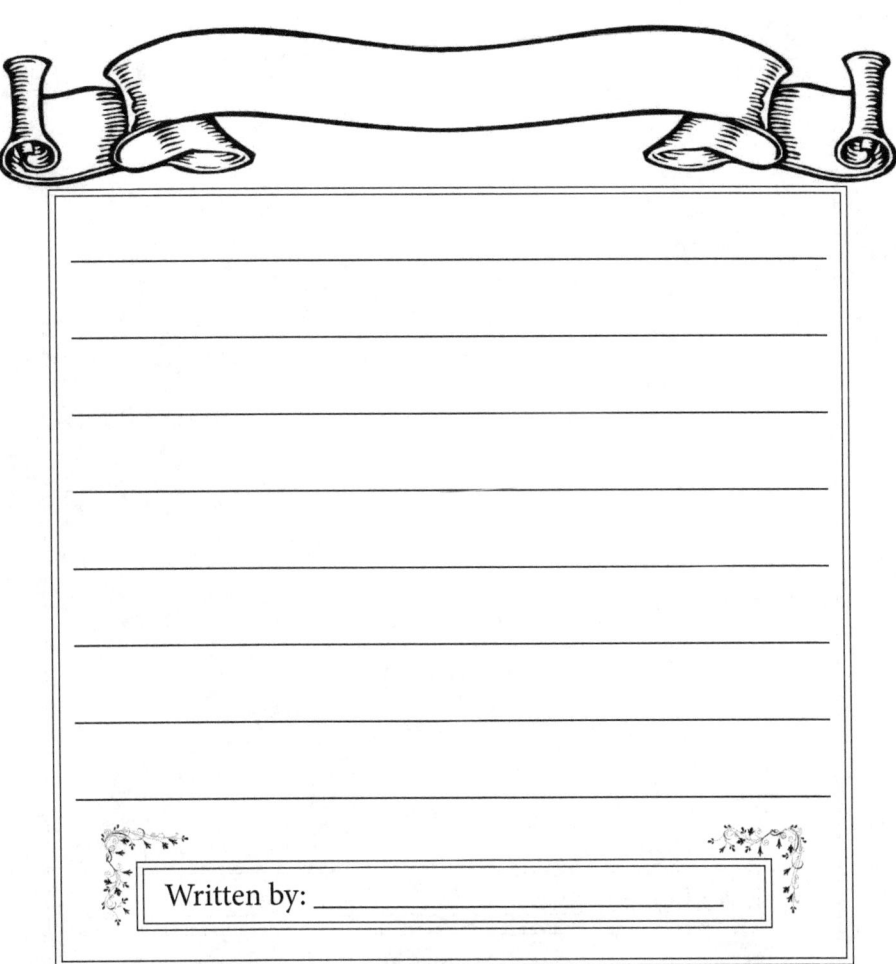

Written by: _____

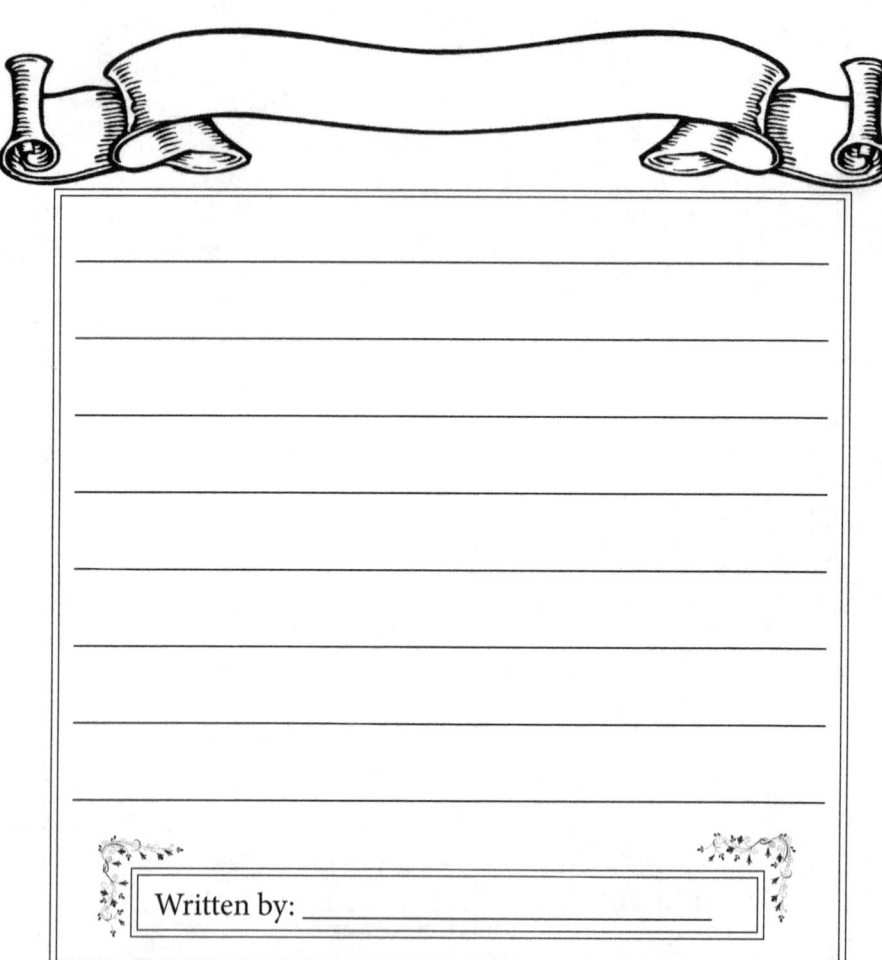

Written by: _____

Written by: _____

Written by: _____

Written by: _____

Written by: _____

Written by: _____

Written by: _____

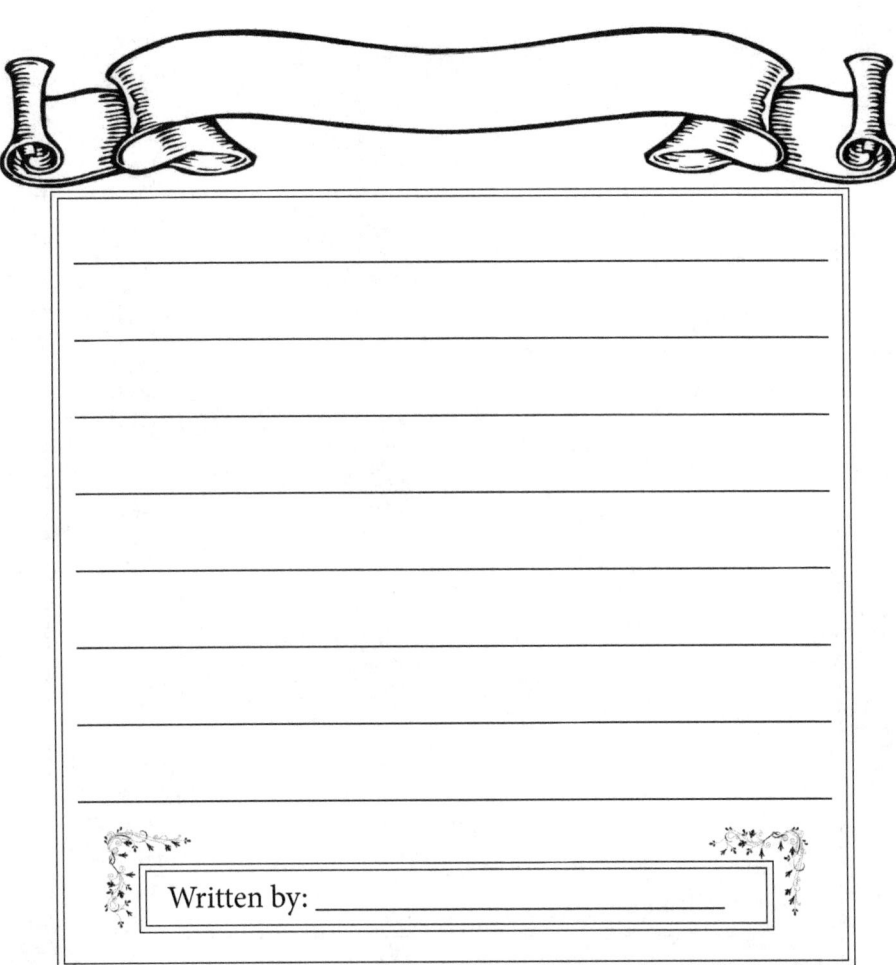

Written by: _____

Written by: _____

Written by: _____

Written by: _____

Written by: _____

Written by: _____

Written by: _____

Written by: _____

Written by: _____

Reflections

About the Publisher

Matrika Press is an independent publishing house dedicated to publishing works in alignment with liberal religious Values and Principles. Its fiscal sponsor is Unitarian Universalist Women and Religion, a 501c3 organization.

Matrika Press publishes anthologies, memoirs, poetry, prayer and ritual manuscripts, and other books to bring meaning and transformation to the world. A primary goal of Matrika Press is to publish stories and works that would otherwise remain untold. We also resurrect out-of-print manuscripts to ensure our historical works remain accessible.

Why the name "Matrika"?
It is said that Matrika is the intrinsic energy or sound vibration of the 50 letters of the Sanskrit alphabet called "the mothers of creation." The Goddess Kali Ma used the letters to form words, and from the words formed all things. This aligns with scriptures that assert "in the beginning was the Word," and in other sacred texts that affirm people of all backgrounds and faiths agree: Words are powerful. More than that: Their vibrations are creative forces; they bring all things into being.

Matrika Press titles are automatically made available to tens of thousands of retailers, libraries, schools, and other distribution and fulfillment partners, including Amazon, Barnes & Noble, Chapters/Indigo (Canada), and other well-known book retailers and wholesalers across North America, and in the United Kingdom, Europe, Australia and New Zealand and other Global partners.

For more information, visit:

www.MatrikaPress.com

About the Author

Rev. Dr. "Twinkle" Marie Porter-Manning is an interfaith minister, skilled ritualist and liturgist who has been leading workshops and seminars in the secular and spiritual worlds for more than two decades. She actively develops and leads programs that nourish spirituality. Her rituals, reflections and poetry have been included internationally in all manner of worship services and publications.

The series of *Blessing Books* is the newest of her publishing endeavors. Other published works include the *Women of Spirit* anthology series, *Intentional Visualization, Be Like the Trees, Restore Us to Memory*, and the *Pulpit of Peace* collection. Upcoming works include the *Sophia* anthologies series, *Anam Ċara and The Divine Echo,* and *Möbius Living as Way of Building The Beloved Community and Healing the Loneliness that Exists in the World.*

Her community ministry, affectionately known as *Twinkle's Place,* has two locations in Maine, USA where she hosts a variety of retreats and spiritual programs.

www.MatrikaPress.com/twinkle-marie-manning
www.MooseheadLakeRetreats.org
www.TwinklesPlace.org

Other Works by this Author

Women of Spirit
of
Spirit

Exploring Sacred Paths of Wisdom Keepers
Compiled and Edited by "Twinkle" Marie Manning
Cover Art by Shiloh Sophia
a Sojourn With Light Workers book

www.MatrikaPress.com/women-of-spirit

Women of Spirit, Exploring Sacred Paths of Wisdom Keepers is a compilation of women sojourners, sages, mystics, witches, shaman, medicine women, ministers, philosophers, therapists, life coaches, yogis, and more.
Their journeys.
Their stories.
Their teachings and practices.
Essays, Poetry, Art, Rituals and Prayers. This anthology is full of useful tools and powerful messages for everyone who is on a spiritual journey to embrace and enjoy. Beloved Contributors include:

- *Anna Huckabee Tull*
- *Bernadette Rombough*
- *Deb Elbaum* • *Deborah Diamond*
- *Debra Wilson Guttas* • *Grace Ventura*
- *Janeen Barnett* • *JoAnne Bassett*
- *Judy Ann Foster* • *Julie Matheson*
- *Kate Early* • *Kate Kavanagh*
- *Katherine Glass* • *Kris Oster*
- *Lea M. Hill* • *Meghan Gilroy*
- *Morwen Two Feathers* • *Rustie MacDonald*
- *Shamanaca* • *Sharon Hinckley*
- *Shawna Allard* • *Shiloh Sophia*
- *Susan Feathers* • *Tiffany Cano*
- *Tory Londergan*
- *"Twinkle" Marie Porter-Manning*
- *Tziporah Kingsbury* • *Valerie Sorrentino*

Pulpit of Peace: *Inspirational Quotes from a Prophetic Ministry*

This book features excerpts from Rev. Dr. "Twinkle" Marie Porter-Manning's sermons, as well as glimpses of her poetry, meditations, rituals and reflections. Common themes of her ministry and writings found in this book include: Building The Beloved Community; Möbius Life; Explorations of Divinity; Living Life as a Prayer.

Pulpit of Peace is part of the *a Pocketful Book Series*.

Be Like the Trees *(a Sermon in My Pocket)* speaks candidly about tragedy, grief, and challenges faced in daily life. Rev. Dr. "Twinkle" Marie Porter-Manning's words weave together a beautiful collage of insights and inspirations as she directs us towards the interconnectedness and magic of our human existence.

Coming Soon...

Möbius Living *as Way of Building The Beloved Community and Healing the Loneliness that Exists in the World*

In its holistic shaping of The Beloved Community, *Möbius Living* teaches us to be vigilant about what we are nurturing from the inside out, and the outside in.

www.MatrikaPress.com

Coming Soon to the "a Sermon in My Pocket" series:

Restore Us to Memory explores remembering (and reclaiming) who we are and offers encouragement to live our lives in such a way that we will be remembered how, and as who, we want to be remembered as.

Anam Ċara and The Divine Echo centers a mystical aspect of belonging, and practical ways to demonstrate such belonging in our lives.

Other Books by Matrika Press

SEA CHANGE:

the unfinished agenda of the 1960s

Dorothy May Emerson

Matrika Press

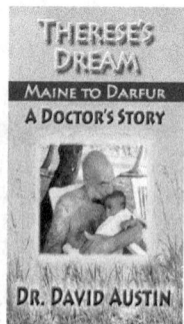

www.MatrikaPress.com

Featured Titles

The Circle Model of
SHARED LEADERSHIP

By Elizabeth Fisher

Sponsored by Unitarian Universalist Women and Religion
& Unitarian Universalist Women's Federation
Published by Matrika Press

The Circle Model of Shared Leadership by Elizabeth Fisher is a concrete group facilitation process that balances achieving tasks with emotional bonding. By using this book you will:

- Learn ways to bring a collection of individuals together, in a committee, board, or activist project, uniting each one's efforts which are equally valued.
- Develop skills critical to honing participatory decision-making and supporting the soul of the group, which must be kept strong if the group is to accomplish its goals.
- Discover important principles, practices and tools that support effective collaboration within and among all the levels of organizations.

www.MatrikaPress.com/the-circle-model

Making A Monster
The first last word on 3D MONSTER design

Sue Roy Humphries

Sue Roy Humphries' historic aggregation work featuring behind-the-scenes documentation of sci-fi and horror classics in theatrical make-up effects has been all but hidden from the world for decades. Originally published in 1980, **Making a Monster** has been long out of print.

Matrika Press is delighted to revive this manuscript on its 40th Anniversary in response to those seeking a comprehensive montage of this highly creative aspect of filmmaking.

Making a Monster reveals the artistic secrets of your favorite vintage fantasy films. This book is filled with detailed accounts of the early era of makeup processes and ingenious solutions to the challenges of pre-CGI Visual FX.

While the manuscript reveals the trade and techniques of transforming some of Hollywood's most beautiful and beloved icons into infamous villains and fantastical creatures, its content also lends a lens unto the human psyche, including that of choosing what to believe in. Said another way, choosing One's Faith.

www.MatrikaPress.com/making-a-monster

Moosehead Lake Retreats
www.MooseheadLakeRetreats.org

Matrika Press

www.MatrikaPress.com

9 781946 088178